Create Your Own Website

Rob Newell
and Nick Ralph

Contents

Introduction	5
Pre-Tutorial Notes	57
Tutorial	65
Uploading your Site	130
Advanced Stuff	138
Glossary	170
Useful Sites	187

INTRODUCTION

If you're reading this, there's a reasonable possibility that you already know that 'Internet' is a word that describes millions of computers all round the world that are in some way connected together; the word Internet itself is a contraction of the term 'interconnected networks'. Some of these computers, known as 'servers', can be accessed by other computers, but most home machines, known as 'clients', will not be available for anyone else to access.

The connecting links take the form of cables of varying capacities, similar to a system of roads that ranges from country lanes to six-lane highways. The rate at which information can be transmitted along the cable is determined by the kind of cable being used. Computers use conventional telephone lines, cable, ISDN (Integrated Services Digital Network), ADSL (Asymmetric Digital Subscriber Line), fibre-optics and, increasingly these days, wireless connections including satellite links. Some of these, for instance ADSL, use conventional copper telephone cables, but in a sophisticated way.

Introduction

The Internet works via a similar principle to the telephone system, although it carries data instead of speech. In fact, a large proportion of home and small-business Internet users connect to the Internet via their telephone line using a modem; larger business users, educational and government establishments will have high-speed, permanent connections. More recently, smaller users have been able to get higher-speed, always-on connection via technologies such as ADSL (which is able to run on normal telephone lines, providing they are of good enough quality and close enough to the telephone exchange) and cable modems (modems that enable you to connect your computer to a cable TV line with a fast connection).

The Internet, or Net as it is often known, has many uses, the primary ones being e-mail and the World Wide Web (WWW). It is used for many other purposes, however, such as newsgroups, file transfer, remote backups and printing, Internet relay chat, and even telephone conversations and conferencing.

The term e-mail is short for electronic mail.

Instead of writing or typing a letter, putting it in an envelope, posting it and then possibly having to wait days or weeks for it to reach its recipient if they're on the other side of the world, you type your message in your e-mail program, connect to the Internet (if you aren't already connected) and press a 'send' button. The message lodges on the recipient's mail server within seconds, or minutes at worst, ready for when the recipient next collects their mail. Larger organizations that have their own mail servers can route the message to the recipient's computer immediately, without them even needing to collect it. These days, many businesses have become extremely reliant on this means of instant communication, and experience nightmare scenarios when their systems are 'down' (not working properly).

The World Wide Web, comprising millions of websites, can be used for a multitude of activities. These range from search and retrieval of all kinds of information, fan websites dedicated to pop and film stars and electronically published magazines and newspapers to online banking, shopping and customer support.

You'll probably be familiar with the term 'web-surfing' – it simply means browsing the Web and taking advantage of all that information out there. It's a vast, worldwide resource. If you can imagine it, it's probably either on the Internet somewhere, or will, like your own website, be there in the not-too-distant future!

So, when did the Internet start? How did it start? Who invented it? And who owns it? Well, no one invented the Internet, it just evolved. And no one owns the Internet, although there are supervisory bodies that set technical standards and allocate/register domain names (e.g. **nasa.gov**; **microsoft.com**; **bbc.co.uk**).

A Brief History of Computing

It's hard to imagine that the Internet could have been developed without the existence of computers. The world could be a very different place without many pioneering inventions although, in many cases, the invention was inevitable and the visionary who invented or discovered it first simply got there ahead of everyone else. Indeed, often, several groundbreaking pioneers were working on similarly enlightened ideas simultaneously. So it is with computers and communications, and the story probably starts with the abacus, the first counting machine, which dates from Egypt around 500 BC.

Nothing significant in the history of computing is known to have happened after that until the 17th century, when a number of mechanical calculating machines, including the circular slide rule, were invented. Probably the most significant of these was the wooden calculating machine devised by

Introduction

Wilhelm Schickard of Tübingen in southern Germany, who came up with the first known mechanical calculator in 1623.

The discovery of electricity in the 18th century, and a slew of inventions and developments including calculators, telegraphy equipment and the typewriter in the 19th century, all contributed to the shape of computers, and modern technology generally, as we know them today. Although his work was largely unknown and therefore was not built upon by others, Charles Babbage was probably the most significant inventor of the 19th century. Babbage's analytical engine of 1833 was the earliest real forerunner of the modern computer. You may not realize it, but the companies that later became Toshiba and IBM were founded in the 19th century.

In the 20th century, technology developed a lot more quickly, and a lot sooner, than many people may realize today. The company that became Motorola was started in 1928 and Hewlett-Packard was founded in 1939. In the late 1930s, the relatively unknown Konsrad Zuse in Berlin, Alan Turing in England and John Atanasoff with John Berry at Iowa State University were all developing what would become modern computing.

During the Second World War, the code-breaking establishment at Bletchley Park, in England, developed Colossus to decrypt messages being sent by the German Enigma coding machine. After the war, the invention of the transistor got things really moving and there were many people simultaneously working on developing new ideas for computers and related technologies.

For more detailed information, check out the following websites:

www.computer.org/history/development
www.computerhope.com/history
www.gris.uni-tuebingen.de/projects/schickard
www.ex.ac.uk/BABBAGE
www.turing.org.uk
turing.net

Introduction

The seeds of the Internet were sown in the late 1950s when, in response to the launch of Sputnik by the USSR, the US government's Advanced Research Projects Agency (ARPA) was established. Throughout the early to mid-1960s, ARPA experimented with connecting computers together over a telephone line, while packet-switching technology was also being developed. The latter was based on the principle of sending of data in packets, just like a letter comprising a few pages in one envelope, where each page would be equivalent to a packet. If one packet was corrupted, or lost, only that small packet would need to be sent again rather than the whole file. Packet-switching was essential for the development of computer networks.

These concepts gathered momentum from 1966 onwards as plans for the ARPANET (the first widespread computer network) were proposed and developed. By 1968, hardware had been commissioned and the first data was transferred the following year. By 1971, there were fifteen academic and military establishments connected together, including Harvard, UCLA (University of California at Los Angeles) and, of course, NASA (National Aeronautics and Space Administration). The first e-mail program was written by Ray Tomlinson of BBN (Bolt Beranek and Newman Inc., who built the first packet-switching devices) in 1971 and the use of the @ symbol was introduced the following year.

The first international connections to the ARPANET were made in 1973; and in 1974, TCP (Transmission Control Protocol) was devised, a means of transferring data that became a fundamental building block of the Internet. (It provides a common protocol, or 'language', that computers can use to communicate across a network.) TCP was trialled by satellite links between Stanford University, California, BBN and University College, London, England.

In the late 1970s, TCP was split into TCP and IP (Internet Protocol) and Usenet (newsgroups) was established. By the end of the decade, the number of host computers on the ARPANET had grown to 188 from just four at the end of the 1960s.

Throughout the 1980s, other computer networks were established, such as France Telecom's Minitel and CSNET (Computer and Science Network, which was developed for academic scientists with no access to ARPANET) and many developments took place that shaped the Internet we know today. In 1982, TCP and IP became the established protocol for transferring data. They were combined and were henceforth referred to as TCP/IP. In the following year, this became the protocol used on all networks. CSNET was linked to ARPANET and whole networks of desktop computers were now starting to become connected instead of there being just a single host computer at each location.

In 1983, one of the most significant developments in computing, something that has made the Internet and the World Wide Web what it is today, took place: the creation of Name Servers. The Domain Name System was introduced the following year. It is these two developments that enable your domain to be known as, for example, **holidayaddicts.com**, as opposed to its IP address, which is a sequence of four numbers separated by full stops – for example, 66.79.10.214 – in which each number can be anything from 0 to 255. When you want to go to the Holiday Addicts website, you only need to know the domain name. This is then 'looked up' on a Domain Name Server, which translates it into the IP address to take you there.

In 1984, the number of connected host computers exceeded 1,000 for the first time. The first domains were registered in spring 1985 and during 1987 the number of hosts reached 10,000. By 1989 they had passed the 100,000 mark and at the end of the decade Australia, Canada, Denmark, Finland, France, Germany, Iceland, Israel, Italy, Japan, Mexico, Norway, the Netherlands, New Zealand, Puerto Rico, Sweden, the United Kingdom and the United States were all connected. Argentina, Austria, Belgium, Brazil, Chile, Greece, India, Ireland, Korea,

Spain and Switzerland joined the next year and ARPANET was closed down. There are now many domain endings (e.g. **.gov**; **.net**; **.com**; **.biz**; **.info**; **.co.uk**), many of which can only be allocated to certain kinds of organizations, and some are more restricted than others.

Back in 1945, Vannevar Bush had foreseen personal computers and the World Wide Web with his hypothetical Memex device. According to Bush, this would be 'a future device for individual use, which is a sort of mechanized private file and library. It . . . is a device in which an individual stores all his books, records and communications, and which is mechanized so that it may be consulted with exceeding speed and flexibility.' It seems he was imagining a computer connected to the Internet and, although the idea of 'exceeding speed' may still seem like something of a pipe dream to web-surfers, the Internet is very fast compared to retrieving data from libraries or via ordinary mail across the world.

Tim Berners-Lee proposed the idea of the World

Wide Web while he was working at the CERN (European Organization for Nuclear Research – **www.cern.ch**) laboratory in Switzerland in 1989. It was actually realized in late 1990 and introduced in 1991. Considering its significance in today's world of communications and technology, the CERN home page carries the somewhat understated tag-line, 'where the Web was born'.

The World Wide Web is based on HTML – Hypertext Markup Language – a fiendishly clever way of presenting information to maximize its content (see page 27 for further explanation). It was based on SGML (Standard Generalized Markup Language), devised by Charles F. Goldfarb way back in 1970. Instead of documents containing references to further information, they contain 'links' (usually called 'hyperlinks') that, when you click on them, actually take you to that new source of information. The latter could be somewhere in the same document, somewhere in another document on the same computer, or in a document on a computer on the other side of the world. Once you've used it, you soon realize how useful this is – and you soon take it for granted.

The World Wide Web is rather like a document delivery service. Through a hyperlink you request a document and it is delivered to your computer screen. Because the Internet has its own protocols, such as TCP/IP, any computer connected to it and running those protocols can use its facilities, whether it's a PC, Apple Macintosh, Unix box, mainframe, PDA (Personal Digital Assistant) or mobile phone.

With the invention of the World Wide Web, combined with the convenience of e-mail that accompanied it, the expansion of the Internet became phenomenal. Throughout the 1990s, more and more countries came onstream and the number of users connected to the Net increased exponentially. Now, if you live in the western world and you have a computer, you're probably connected to the Internet.

If you're interested in how the World Wide Web

was developed and how it works, check out **www.zakon.org/robert/Internet/timeline** for a history of how the Internet came about and **http://public.web.cern.ch/Public/ACHIEVEMENTS/web.html** for the story of how HTML was born.

Most people just use the Internet for e-mail and surfing/web-browsing– so what's the difference?

Well, e-mail – electronic mail – is quite literally what it says it is. It's just like conventional post (or, as it's now known, snail mail), except that it can happen almost instantaneously. You have an address – yourname@yourdomain – and you can send mail to anyone else who also has an e-mail address, but the whole process takes seconds rather than days.

Although you use the same equipment and medium (your computer and the Internet), web-browsing is the electronic equivalent of visiting the best-stocked library in the world, or maybe visiting your local shopping mall or bank. If it's something you can do without physically being there, the kind of thing you could do over the phone, then you can probably do it at a website! You can search for and retrieve documents, buy goods by mail order, check your bank balance and make payments from your account on the Web, amongst many other things.

No doubt about it, the Internet has dramatically changed the way we live. For instance, there are millions of people in the world who share the name Smith, but there can only be one smith.com. In the early days, this domain-name exclusivity encouraged a phenomenon known as cybersquatting. While big companies were yet to embrace the idea and potential of the Internet, students were registering their names, or other significant sequences of letters, as 'dotcoms' (e.g. coke.com, amex.com) in the hope that the companies who were interested in these names would pay large amounts to regain them. Some did, but these days cybersquatters are being taken to court to relinquish these names, as they could be said to be 'passing themselves off' as someone they weren't by registering them.

There is now a plethora of magazines devoted to computers and the Internet. Just look in your local newsagent and compare the number of computer and Internet magazines to those devoted to other pursuits – it's breeding jargon like it's going out of fashion! HTML, CGI, WAP, WYSIWYG . . . what does it all mean? See the end of this book for enlightenment!

It's worth bearing one thing in mind before you even start thinking about building a website of your own. The computer platform you are on (PC or Mac) and the browser you are using (Explorer, Netscape or Opera, for example) may well determine the way that a website appears on your screen. Professional web-developers test their websites with different browsers on different platforms to try and achieve a consistent experience for visitors to the site, but it's inevitable that there will be differences. All you can hope for is that at least your site makes sense in all browsers on all platforms, although it probably won't look exactly the same on all of them.

The Internet is constantly evolving as software and hardware are developed and updated. A number of items had to be revised throughout the writing of this book and, inevitably, some information may have been superseded by the time you are reading it . . .

What is a website?

A website is like a magazine, but it is accessed electronically, usually on a computer. It can also be an encyclopedia, a searchable database, a chatroom, an online shop or a means of accessing your bank account. A website sits on a web-server waiting for people to go and look at it. It usually consists of a number of pages linked to one other. These pages can contain text, information, pictures, graphics, animations, sound, guest books and even movie clips. Most sites are created by end-users like you, and can be seen by millions of people all around the world.

The majority of the time, websites are free to visit. If you have access to the Internet then you will probably have access to some web space for a website!

What do you want from your website?

You can use it for your business, to promote products or services or for customer support. You may want to have an e-commerce site to sell your products online. Not all Internet Service Providers (the companies that give you access to the Internet and provide you with Internet-related services) can support e-commerce, however. Moreover, you would also need to be paying business rates for this kind of site.

You might want a website for personal reasons – for example, to keep family members and distant relatives up to date with your latest news. Or perhaps you have a passion about a hobby, such as stamp collecting, rebuilding old cars or going on holiday, that you'd like to share with others. There are also many fan sites on the Web, mini virtual shrines to movie stars, pop groups and the like.

Then there are sites that exist purely to disseminate information, perhaps for a particular town or area, museum or gallery. Most organizations of any significance have an informative website. You'd be amazed what you can find on the Web.

Whatever a website is used for, it can easily be updated and kept current because of its electronic nature – unlike printed material. In fact, many websites are now set up to be easily updateable by people with limited computing skills, so technically challenged staff can put the latest news stories on to a website, or amend existing ones, without needing to be web wizards or have any knowledge of how to create a website!

Different kinds of sites are suitable for different purposes. Most sites use conventional pages linked together in straightforward HTML. Business and e-commerce sites are more likely to be database-driven. You can tell these from the kind of page names that come up in your browser when you are surfing. Ordinary pages will have a comprehensible file path and name, whereas on database-driven sites it's often a string of complete gobbledygook! You can also tell database-driven sites from the file name endings, such as **.asp**, **.php** and **.ibc**. These endings reveal the programming language used for the site.

The page

A web page is built around HTML. This is a standard text file that includes specific commands to control text and other elements incorporated into the web page. The commands are all incorporated within Tags (see below for further information about these).

Although when you view a web page it looks like one complete document, it is actually made from two main elements, known as the head and body elements. The head element stores information on how to draw (or render) the page in a browser. Information on which character sets to use, any scripting languages that you have used (e.g. JavaScript), information about the contents of the page, who wrote the page and other related material are all stored in the head. The content of your page is all contained within the body; text, links and commands to display images are all stored within the body section.

Tags are made up of normal text surrounded by a < (less-than sign) and a > (greater-than sign). These instruct the web browser to undertake a specific command. When you are using a word processor and you highlight a body of text to become bold, the word processor emboldens the text and hides any commands 'behind the scenes' so that you can't see them. HTML does the same. For instance, it might create the following:

Holidayaddicts.com

This would then display in a browser in bold.

Let's look at the above line more closely. The line starts by creating the bold Tag. This is represented by . Any text placed after this Tag will be shown in a bold typeface. The line is then ended with the Tag. This tells the browser to stop using the bold typeface and return to the normal font. Tags control everything in an HTML document, from what type-faces to use, their styles, sizes and alignment, to how images are placed on a page and the size at which they are to be displayed. You can find a more detailed list of HTML Tags at **www.w3.org** – this is the home of the World Wide Web organization that sets the standards for HTML.

At this point, you may be worrying that you will have to code your web page by hand, as if you were a computer programmer! But fear not, help is at hand. Although you can code your page manually (it can be achieved using a simple package such as Word-Pad for PCs or SimpleText for Macs) we are going to talk you through creating your page in Netscape Communicator. This is a WYSIWYG editor, which enables you to see your web page being created in front of you. (See the section 'WYSIWYG or not WYSIWYG?' on page 35 for further information.)

Basic layout

The most important thing to remember when designing web pages is to keep them simple and uncomplicated. Because you do not know the connection speed a visitor will be using to browse your website, you will need to keep the site lean to make sure that pages load in the quickest time possible. Visitors will soon give up and go elsewhere if your page is still loading after a couple of minutes! Therefore, make sure that any graphics you use are as small as they can be and are only 72dpi (dots per inch) in resolution. Anything higher than this is a waste of time, as a computer screen can only display a maximum of 72dpi. It's also a good idea not to overload your page with lots of different animations, sound clips and movies.

Keep page content to a minimum and only include the relevant information about that section on the page. If you start to waffle you may well lose the reader's interest and they will look elsewhere for the information. If you want to include more detailed information or large animations, you can always link to another page (preferably warning any visitors that the link they are about to click on may take a little while to load). That way, if the user wants to wait for the information to download, it's their choice.

Keep the layout simple and easy to read. If a user is greeted with a lot of different typefaces, in various colours and sizes, it will soon put them off reading your site. Try to keep the initial pages, especially the home page, limited in size so that each fills just one screen, otherwise the user will have to scroll left and right and up and down to get the full information or links to other pages.

Once you have captured the user's interest and linked on to additional pages, you may add more content. The user will scroll up and down once they have entered a page of information, as they will be interested in the content. If they were not interested then they would not have clicked on the link.

Typefaces

With printed material you can specify the typefaces required, print them and distribute them so that the person sees the document exactly as you intended them to. With web pages it's a slightly different procedure; you may create your page around a certain typeface, but unless the user has the same font installed on their computer, the text on the web page will not be displayed as you intended it to be. (If the user's computer doesn't have the specified font installed, their browser will normally default to the system font, which will be Times, Times New Roman, Arial or Helvetica.) HTML offers you the ability to specify a number of font options. Take the following Tag, for example:

<font name="Verdana, Arial, Helvetica, sans-serif">Holidayaddicts.com</font>

The above line displays the text Holidayaddicts.com. It tells the browser to search for the font Verdana.

If that's not present, it tells the browser to look for Arial, and if that's not present it tells the browser to look for Helvetica. If the browser can't find any of the typefaces listed, it will default to a font that has been assigned by the system as a sans-serif typeface (i.e. the simplest form of a typeface, without any extra lines at the extremities of a character).

Although this is not a foolproof method, it does ensure that the page is displayed as closely as possible to the way the page was designed to look. If you use common fonts within your design (e.g. Verdana, Arial, Times, Helvetica) the user will almost certainly have these installed and so should see the page as you intended. If you want to use a particularly unusual typeface, perhaps as a heading or as part of a logo, you should create it as a graphic.

Formatting

You have a basic level of control in formatting your page. You can align items left, centre or right. You can create more advanced pages with columns for text and graphics. The best way to do this is to utilize the HTML Table feature. (This is explained in more detail both within the tutorial and the advanced section towards the end of this book.) Another way of formatting your text, or page, is to use Cascading Style Sheets (CSS). This allows you to customize certain HTML Tags, although as a beginner to creating web pages we would suggest you acquaint yourself with basic pages before attempting anything with CSS. It's certainly beyond the scope of this book.

Look at what others have done!

The web is a vast mass of creativity. A lot of people have built pages, many probably very similar to the kind that you want to build. To help you out, you can find out how someone else's page has been written, via your Internet browser. If you are using Microsoft Internet Explorer, right-click on your mouse button and select View Source (PC users) or click and hold down your mouse button and select View Source (Macintosh users). Within Netscape you can right-click your mouse button and select View Page Source (PC users) or click and hold down your mouse button and select Page Source (Macintosh users). Alternatively, you can find the command under the browser's View menu.

This will open a window with the HTML code in it, enabling you to see how the page, or a particular feature on it, has been created. You can also open someone else's page in the Composer part of Netscape and play with it! In fact, if you find a page with a similar structure to one you want to create, you could open that page in Composer and substitute elements of the page with your own, change the text to your own text and thereby create a page very quickly! However, be careful not to steal anyone else's creative work and infringe their copyright.

WYSIWYG or not WYSIWYG?

WYSIWYG (What You See Is What You Get, pronounced 'wizzywig') is at the heart of the way most word processors and desktop publishing programs work, and is probably the easiest way to build your web pages. It allows you to add images or edit your text and actually see the changes to the page happening in front of you. This ensures that the way you see the page will be as close as possible to the way visitors to your site will see it.

You can build your page in a code editor (or text editor such as WordPad or SimpleText). If you use this route you will have to build the page by hand-coding all of the HTML for every detail you wish to add to it. Should you want to preview the page you have created, you will have to load the page into a web browser to see it. If you then want to make any changes, you will have to revert back to the code editor, make the changes and go back to the preview again to see the results. It's a long-winded process to write HTML pages this way.

With this in mind, we have built our tutorial around a WYSIWYG editor, as it will add all of the HTML Tags and commands for you without the need for you to know any HTML.

File names

When you are dealing with files that are connected with the Web, there are a couple of things to bear in mind. The first is that the file has to end with a suffix. If you create a JPEG graphic image, when you come to save it you will have to name it in the format **picture.jpg**. This then tells the browser that the file is a JPEG graphic file. (This process is not usually required on a Macintosh as they work in a slightly more intelligent way than PCs!) The same principle is required with all files used on the Web. The following table illustrates some common file suffixes:

HTML file	.htm or .html
JPEG file	.jpg
GIF file	.gif
PDF file	.pdf
Text file	.txt
Flash movie	.swf
Quick Time movie	.mov

These are just an illustration of what is available. If you're using a PC, then these suffixes are automatically added to the file when you save them. If you're using a Macintosh, you will have to ensure that you add them, as many applications do not!

The only file type that is an exception to this rule is an HTML file. It can be named .htm or .html – it makes no difference to a web server which variation is used. Make sure whatever route you take (.htm or .html) is used consistently throughout your site, however. This will ensure that things do not get confused at a later stage!

When you save your file, you will also have to be careful which characters you use for the file name. Because addresses on the Web include forward slashes (/), dots (.) and colons (:), you cannot include these in your file name, otherwise the browser will not be able to find the correct file. The best practice to adopt is to keep your file names short (under twelve characters if possible). If you want to add a space to the file name, use an underscore (_) rather than a space. It's also advisable to keep the file names alphanumeric (just numbers and the 26 letters of the alphabet), without special or accented characters or punctuation. The page that you create as your home page will have to be called something like **home.htm** or **index.htm** (or, in either case, **.html**), to ensure that this page is displayed first when somebody types in your Internet address. (See the tutorial for further details.)

Graphics

Although the Internet started life as a text-based medium, it has grown rapidly over the past few years into a graphical-based showcase. This has made it possible to create something much more appealing to look at than a page full of nothing but text.

There are many types of graphics packages available, all with their own proprietary file formats (i.e. specific to the particular application program) and some common ones (e.g. Tiff and EPS), but when it comes to the Internet there is a choice of just two cross-platform formats. Because you are not in control of the platform your visitors are using (Windows, Macintosh or Unix), you will have to use a format that can be interpreted by all platforms. If you were to use a format that only one platform supports, not everyone would be able to view your site as you intended.

Formats

GIF format

GIF stands for 'Graphics Interchange Format'. This was originally created by CompuServe and dates back to the late 1980s. GIFs are bare bitmapped-based images: each pixel (the smallest element of a picture) is mapped to a colour, and in turn all the pixels build up to form the image.

A GIF can only save 256 'indexed' colours from those present in a picture. It 'indexes' the 'best' 256 colours (unless confined to a particular palette, such as Web Safe colours, see page 48) for a particular image. Any colours not represented will be 'dithered'. This means if a particular colour needed is not included in the 256, the image will be saved with pixels coloured to average out to the one required. For example, if orange were required, the file would be saved with red and yellow pixels adjacent to one another so that the eye 'averaged' them out to see orange overall (the eye can be quite easily fooled up to a point!).

GIF also provides the facility to make certain colours within the image transparent. This allows you to overlay a number of graphics without the background obscuring an underlying image (see example below).

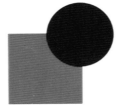

Transparent

Nontransparent

The other advantage of using GIFs is that you can animate them. This allows you to build a series of frames, each with a different image on it, which in turn enables you to build up a 'flick book' form of animation. By adding animated GIFs, you can enhance your site to make it look less static. You do not require any additional plug-in or add-ons to view animated GIFs, unlike other animated files.

GIFs are best used for features such as graphical buttons, logos and advertising banners.

JPEG format

JPEG stands for 'Joint Photographic Experts Group' and is the other widely used graphical format. The most common use for JPEGs is to represent photographic style (continuous tone) pictures. These are pictures that have a relatively broad range of the colour spectrum (millions of colours, allowing an extensive range of tones and hues), as opposed to GIF Format, although they're still bitmapped.

When saving JPEG image files you can specify

how much you would like the files to be compressed. If you save a file with no compression, you retain a high-quality image, with a relatively high file size. High-quality images might look great on the screen, but they could make your website take·a relatively long time to load in a browser window.

Different image-editing programs offer a variety of options when saving JPEGs. You can specify the level of compression – a highly compressed image will reduce the file size, but also the quality. Different applications have their own individual ways of implementing this. By way of illustrating this point, we have used Adobe Photoshop and saved a file at both maximum and low quality (see examples below).

90 x 60mm 72dpi, 100%-quality (lossless) JPEG – 21K file

Introduction

90 x 60mm 72dpi, low-quality JPEG – 6K file

90 x 60mm 72dpi, GIF – 19K file

In the final analysis, it will be up to you to play around with file compression and see for yourself how the quality of the image is affected. You will probably find an acceptable compromise that provides you with both a good-quality image and a relatively small file size. Note: although JPEGs are excellent for photographic images, they don't allow for transparency or animation. And even if an image is saved as a JPEG in millions of colours, it will still be dithered on a screen that can only display 256 colours.

It is important to remember that you can place as many images on your web page as you wish, but even if they are all quite small, the combined size will increase the download time significantly, especially for people with slower connections. You will have to find the right balance with the correct file types, compression of images and the number of images included within your page. As an example, let's consider the picture we have shown above saved at different levels of compression. If there were ten similar pictures on a page, saving the images at the maximum quality as opposed to low-quality JPEGs would mean an extra 150K to download, almost three times as much!

If you save an image as a GIF file, you will lose a lot of the subtlety and sharpness in the image. If a colour in the image is not included in the limited 216-colour Web Safe palette (see page 48), it will be of necessity dithered. What is worse is that the file size won't be much less than a lossless JPEG, which will retain all the colour information. A JPEG saved in low quality could look as good as a GIF although the file is only a quarter of the size!

You can see from the samples shown that there is little benefit to be gained in terms of file size by converting a photographic image to a GIF file as opposed to a lossless JPEG. The savings can be much greater with higher compression JPEGs, and without a great loss of image quality. Different images will look worse with greater compression, depending on their content. Some images will survive the higher levels of compression much better than others. You can only tell how far you can push it by trial and error on a specific image.

It is important to save JPEG files for web use as RGB (red, green and blue) – browsers cannot read CMYK (cyan, magenta, yellow and black) JPEGs.

Web Safe colours

One of the first aspects to consider when designing graphics for the Web is that graphics should ideally be based on a palette that uses 216 colours. Normally the minimum colour palette that a computer uses is based on 256 colours. The main reason for the reduced number of colours is so that all graphics created for the Web can be displayed consistently between Windows, Macintosh and Unix platforms.

Why does this happen? This discrepancy is analogous to what happens when a Windows user opens a text document created on a Macintosh (or vice versa) and sees a lot of odd characters in place of punctuation marks or special characters. (More sophisticated file formats such as Word documents and PDFs convert the characters before you see them.) While the basic characters occupy the same location on the character map, each computer platform places the extended characters (curly quotes, bullet points etc.) in different locations. So, a bullet point on a Macintosh is a Yen (¥) symbol on a Windows machine.

Introduction

The same principle applies to colours. What may display in Windows as grey might display as pale blue on a Macintosh. In the same way that there are basic, common characters, there are basic, common colours between the platforms. These are known as Web Safe colours.

Web Safe colours are made up in terms of RGB values of 0, 51, 102, 153, 204 and 255 (RGB refers to the way the colour is made up on a monitor). These numbers may seem odd numbers to choose, but there is a reason for it! The 255 comes from the fact that the 256 bits are numbered from 0 to 255. Each of the 256 steps for each of the colours, is used for continuous tone (millions of colours) rendering, but in this case, there can only be six options for each colour, 0%, 20%, 40%, 60%, 80%, 100%. Six possibilities for each colour yields 6 x 6 x 6 = 216 permutations, the web palette!

If you are saving in GIF format, ensure that, depending on the software you are using (different applications will have alternative options), you save the GIF using a Web Safe colour palette. With many everyday applications, especially those specializing in creating material for the Web, you do not have to worry about whether the colour you are using is Web Safe – they will do it automatically.

If you want to go into the subject of Web Safe colours in greater detail, Gary W. Priester has it all in depth at **http://www.webdevelopersjournal.com/ articles/websafe1/websafe_colors.html**.

Objects

Horizontal rules

HTML gives you the facility to divide your web document into sections by using horizontal rules. Rules are an excellent tool for dividing your page into sections without adding to the download time. You can insert a horizontal rule into your page at any point, but you can't place images or text on the same line. You can control the thickness of your rule (in pixels or a percentage of the width of the page), give the rule shading, or alter its alignment (left, right or centred).

Lists

Lists are used in both web material and printed material. They provide an easy means of displaying information, displaying points or cataloguing items. HTML gives you the option of using unordered lists or numbered lists.

Unordered Lists – these are lists with bullet points at the start of each item (as you would find on a word processor). You can use an unordered list for displaying a summary of a chapter in a book (see picture below).

This is an example of an Unordered List in HTML

- This is the first line
- This is the second line
- This is the third line etc... etc...

Numbered Lists (or Ordered Lists) – these are very similar to an unordered list, but instead of using a bullet point they use numbers. You could use a numbered list for creating a set of instructions for someone (see picture below).

This is an example of a Numbered (Ordered) List in HTML

1 This is the first line
2 This is the second line
3 This is the third line etc... etc...

You can access lists from Netscape by clicking on the xyz icon for an unordered list and the 123 icon for a numbered list. You can start a list from scratch by clicking on one of these icons and typing your items. Every time you press the Return key, a new bullet or number will appear. When you have finished your list, press the Return key twice to return to your normal text style. Alternatively, you can highlight a selection of text and then click on the relevant icon; this will then change the highlighted text into the relevant list.

Links

Links are used to indicate a relationship between one document and another. So, for example, if web-surfers visit your site and click on a button named 'Venice Holiday', you can direct them to a page dedicated to a trip you took to Venice. Links are used within a website to link the documents together and so provide users with the quickest route to the information they are looking for.

You are not restricted to just linking files on your

own site. You can also link users to any other web page on the Internet. For example, if you decide to create a web page around a certain make of car, you may wish to have a link on your page to the manufacturer's website, or to other people who have created similar web pages. Instead of pointing the link to the page that you have created, you point the link to the website address (e.g. **www.car-manufacturer. com/the-same-model-as-mine.htm**).

You can also make links to picture files, so that when someone clicks on a link, a picture opens up in their browser window. Other items that you can link to include video clips, Flash movies, applications and PDF files. The user may require additional plug-in modules for their browser if you link certain types of file (plug-ins are additional software that add to your existing software's functions).

Links also enable you to open a blank e-mail with a predetermined e-mail address in it. This saves you having to copy the e-mail address from the browser to the e-mail software. Instead of pointing the link at another HTML file or image, you simply point the link to **mailto:youre-mailaddress@yourdomainname** instead. This will then automatically open the user's e-mail program with the above e-mail address in the 'to' (or 'address') field.

Design and the need for speed

Finally, here are a few golden rules to bear in mind when you're designing your own website:

- Keep it simple. 'Less is more', to quote an old design adage. Make your pages easy to navigate and remove all unnecessary clutter.
- Remember, you're producing a document for the Web, not a printed page – they are different!
- Do whatever you can to keep your pages as small as possible. Speed is everything.
- Remember, the World Wide Web is international. Don't be unnecessarily parochial.
- Be wary of the latest technology – most users won't be that up-to-date. Avoid new technologies that

won't work on older systems, especially those that won't display anything at all!

If you are intending to use the tutorial to construct a website you intend to put on the Internet, please check with your service provider as to the way in which you have to name your home page.

PRE-TUTORIAL
NOTES

1. Before beginning the tutorial we would advise you to create a new folder where you will save all of the files created for your website. This can be located anywhere on your hard drive (just remember where you've saved it!). For the purposes of the tutorial, we have created a folder called webpages, but you could just as easily name it website or anything else of your choice. To make things easier, it is good practice to organize the information that you are going to save into this folder, so after creating the folder webpages, create a new folder inside it called images. This is where you will store all the graphic images that you will use for your site. When you look inside your webpages folder on a PC you should have a window similar to the one in fig. 1. On a Mac you will just see the images folder. It's important to save the files for a website together in a simple structure and then not to move or re-name them, as once you've made links between them, a web browser looks for the name of the file and the location of one file relative to another.

Fig. 1

2. Before starting to construct your website, we would recommend that you create or acquire any graphics or pictures that you are going to use and save or copy them into the images folder. This will then allow you to create your page in one hit without having to switch between applications. For the purposes of this tutorial we have already scanned our photographs and created our graphical navigation buttons.

If you want to work through this tutorial, but

don't yet have any graphics or photographs of your own to work with, we recommend that you either use some of the many public domain and free samples provided on give-away CDs available with computer magazines or download some from the Internet (see the list of useful websites at the back of this book). Alternatively, if you want to work though the tutorial and follow step by step, you can visit the **holidayaddicts.com** website and download the actual files that we have used. It is advisable to name files in a descriptive way, so that you know what each one is by its name.

3. Because it's free and easy to obtain, we are going to use the Composer part of Netscape Communicator to create our website. This is available for both Macintosh and PC platforms and will also allow you to upload your finished site to your Internet server. The software is available as a free download from **www.netscape.com** and other websites, or you can find it on most free computer magazine CDs. You can also create a website with Netscape Navigator, but note that from version 6 onwards, the facility to upload your site is not implemented.

By default, the preferences set in Composer will cause a copy of a placed picture or graphic to be saved in the same folder as the web page it is placed on, and it is this copy that is referenced by the HTML code. If you want to have your files saved in your own organized hierarchy, created before you started, it is a good idea to change this setting. You do this by going to the Edit menu, then

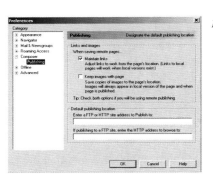

Fig. 2

to Preferences. In the Preferences box that appears, select Publishing (Publish on a Mac) and then uncheck the 'Keep images with page box' (see fig. 2). If you do not do this, all your files will have to be loose in the same folder (not recommended, especially as a website gets larger and more complicated as you add to it) unless you manually check 'Leave image at the original location' each time you place a picture or graphic on a page.

4. The tutorial is based around developing the pages on a PC, but references to developing them on a Macintosh, where there are significant differences between the two systems, are also included. The content is essentially the same on both platforms; the only difference is in the way that the windows are displayed and in the way some of the functions are accessed. Fig. 3 shows the blank window that opens when you create a new file on a PC. Fig. 4 shows how it would appear on a Macintosh. As you can see, the main difference is the window that the document is contained in, particularly the top

Pre-Tutorial Notes

Fig. 3

Fig. 4

bar, window resizing options and the scroll bars. You will also notice that on a Macintosh, the toolbar icons are not labelled with their function; but if you hold the pointer over an icon, a little label of its function will pop up underneath. Also, on a Macintosh, Properties are named either Info or Format.

5. We are going to show you how to create some simple pages with text, pictures and navigational buttons. There are many other features and properties that you can set in the windows that are shown. A good way to learn about these options is to experiment with them.

6. If you are about to use the tutorial to construct a website you intend to put on the Internet, please check with your web space provider what you have to name your home page (see panel 'Naming Your Home Page', on pages 86–87).

TUTORIAL

Fig. 5

Fig. 5 is the completed home page we are going to create in this tutorial, a basic web page that includes some styled text, a table, an image, a text link and some buttons with links.

Tutorial

1. After you've launched Netscape Communicator, it will open into a browser window as if you were surfing the Net. Under the Communicator menu you will find the option Composer. Composer is the part of Netscape Communicator (and Navigator) that has the capability to create web pages. When you choose this option it will open a

Fig. 6

blank document. Alternatively, you can go to the File menu and choose New, then Blank Page from the sub-menu. This is the start of your web page (see figs 3 and 4).

2. You can now start to type text on to the page (see fig. 6, page 67), in the same way that you would type in text using a word processor.

Type in the title of the page, which in this case is 'Holidayaddicts.com'. Now you can start to style the text that you have just typed in. Highlight the text, and make the text size 36. (Font sizes in HTML are not denoted by point sizes as we are used to in word processors or DTP applications. Most of us are familiar with, say, 10pt as a text size and, say, 24 or 36pt for a heading. Composer tries to be more user-friendly by offering sizes that approximate to point sizes we are familiar with, such as 36. This will convert to +4 in HTML, which to most people means nothing, whereas 36 gives a better idea of the size you might expect.)

By using the buttons to the right of the Text

Size box, you can start to apply colours and different styles to the highlighted text.

If you are using a PC, then you will notice a button to indicate text colour on the toolbar. On a Macintosh the icon is different. If you click on the button (PC), you will get a drop-down palette (fig. 7, page 70), from which you can select the colour that you would like the text to be. If you click on the button marked Other . . ., you can then mix a custom colour of your choice (fig. 8, page 70). But beware, on a PC you do not get a Web Safe colour option, so your chosen custom colour may not display as you would wish on all systems.

On a Macintosh you will be given a Colour Picker window. Scroll down the window on the left-hand side, until you come to the icon marked HTML Picker. Click on this and you will now be able to mix your chosen colour in the right-hand side of the window (fig. 9, page 71). It is advisable to have the 'Snap to Web colour' box checked so that you are using a colour that will display

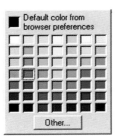

Fig. 7

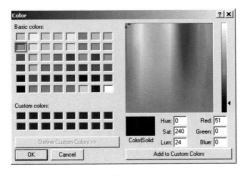

Fig. 8

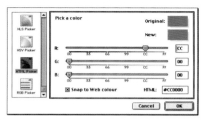

Fig. 9

consistently on all systems. When you are happy with the colour, click OK. In the illustration shown, we have chosen to colour the text red.

Now that you have changed the colour, alter the alignment of the text. By using the Text Align icon, you can choose to align the selected text left, right or centred. For our page we are going to centre the title, so select the second option in the list, the icon showing centred lines.

You can also change the font in which the text is displayed. To do this on a PC, first find the drop-down menu that contains the title Variable Width.

If you click on the arrow to the right of this it will give you a menu of all the fonts installed on your computer. You can select any font that you have available from your list, or the default variable- or fixed-width fonts. As we mentioned previously in the book, be careful which fonts you use in your web page.

Changing the font on a Macintosh involves a

Fixed- vs variable-width fonts

The difference between a fixed-width font (monospace) and a variable-width font is the amount of space a character takes up along the line of text. In a fixed-width font, the kind of font that you find on a typewriter, all the characters occupy the same space horizontally, so an 'i' or an 'l', or even an apostrophe, will take up as much room on the line as an 'm' or 'w'. This can look ugly, especially in sans-serif fonts, although even in serif fonts, such as Courier, it's less than ideal. The narrow letters always look as though there's too much space around slightly different process. If you look under the Format menu, then Font, you will be given a list of your installed fonts. We have chosen to leave the font as the default variable width.

If you hold your pointer over any icon in the toolbar, Netscape Composer will display a small help bubble telling you what that icon does, although if you have used a word processor you

---

them and the wider letters always look cramped.

In a variable-width font, each letter is allocated space related to its appearance, so in equivalent terms, an 'n' may take up twice as much space as an 'i' and an 'm' may take up three times as much space. However, most fonts will have a fixed width for the numerals, so that they'll line up in tables, arithmetic and accounts.

Generally, a variable-width font will look better than a fixed-width font, but there are occasionally times when a fixed-width font is preferable, especially if you want text to line up to look neat or symmetrical.

will probably recognize most of the icons. If you make a mistake or want to go back to the default text style for what you typed in, you can click on the Remove All Styles icon to remove any changes or styles that you have applied.

3. Now we are going to insert a horizontal line underneath the title. This will separate the title from the rest of the page and make it easier for people looking at the page to distinguish between the title and the content. To insert the horizontal line, insert a Return to move the cursor to the next line, then click on the Horizontal Line icon. This will then insert the line automatically. If you want to insert a horizontal line in between two existing blocks of text, you need to place your cursor on the line where you want the horizontal line to be.

You can change the settings of this line by double-clicking on the line. This will then bring up a Horizontal Line Properties window (Horizontal Line Info on a Mac) that will allow you to modify the settings of this line (see fig. 10). If you have

Fig. 10

more than one horizontal line inserted on your page, you will have to double-click and change the settings on each line individually.

From the Horizontal Line Properties window you can change aspects of the line's appearance such as its height (thickness), whether the length of the line is to be a percentage size of the open window or a fixed size (in pixels) and the alignment of the line. You can even add 3-D shading to the line if you wish. You will notice a tick box that saves the current settings as the default for any line you subsequently create.

If you have already created one horizontal line in your document and want to create more lines identical to the first without having to remember the settings and change them each time, enter the Properties box, make your changes and ensure that the default settings box is ticked. If you then insert any more horizontal lines into your page they will be created with the same settings as your first line.

4. You are now going to insert a table into your page. Although you would normally expect to use a table to display data, such as figures, it will also allow us to place an image under the title with the text content positioned to the right of the image.

You will have to insert a Return to move your cursor to the line underneath the horizontal line that you have just created. Once it is there, click on the Table icon in the toolbar.

A Table Properties box (Table Info for Macs) will now appear on the screen. From here you can start to specify the characteristics of the table that you are about to insert. For the purposes of this tutorial, you will need to insert a table that is going

Fig. 11

to be 1 row in height and 2 columns in width. If the default settings are different in the Properties box that appears, then change them accordingly (fig. 11).

As you can see, you can also change a number of properties relating to the table that is about to be created. As you are using the table to lay out the page (i.e. to place the image to one side of the text), you do not want any borders around the table or its cells. You can turn off this option by making sure the box next to the Border Line Width option is not checked.

Click OK and the table will be created where the cursor was positioned.

The table is shown in your page as a black dotted line around your cells. Next you can start to insert information into these cells.

5. You can now insert the image into the left-hand cell of your table and some text into the right-hand cell. Start by typing text into the right-hand side of the table (if you wish, you can copy the text as seen in fig. 15). As you type you will notice that the cell starts to expand, reducing the size of the left-hand cell. This is because you have not set up any fixed size for either cell. Type your text, then right-click (PC) and look for the option Table Properties, or hold the mouse button down (Macintosh) and look for the option Table Info. This will then bring up the Properties window (Format on a Mac) for the cell that your cursor is in. Make sure that the Cell tab is selected at the top of the window. You can now specify the characteristics of that cell (fig. 12).

Fig. 12

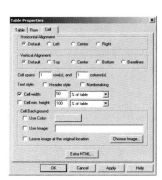

Fig. 13

You will notice the option of Cell Width halfway down the window. Click on the Cell Width tick box and set it to 50% (fig. 13, page 79). This will mean that the cell will only occupy 50% of the table width. After you have clicked OK, the table is resized to the value set.

Next you will need to insert the picture into the left-hand side. To do this, place your cursor in the left-hand cell of the table and click on the Image icon in the toolbar. This will bring up an Image Properties box (Format for Macs). From here you

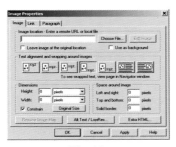

Fig. 14

can specify settings of the picture and which picture you would like to place on the page.

To insert the required picture, click on the button 'Choose file' (fig. 14). This will then bring up a standard open/save dialog window. You can now locate the file that is saved inside the **images** folder, within the **webpages** folder that you created earlier. Once you have found the picture, click on Open. (We have chosen the image **the_hol_addicts.jpg**.)

You are then returned to the Image Properties window (fig. 14), or Format window for Macs. As you can see, you can also specify any changes you'd like to make, such as altering the dimensions of the image or putting space around it. For now, all you'll need to do is insert the image. Before clicking OK, if you want to retain your folder structure for your website and you haven't changed the default preferences as described in the pre-tutorial notes, you will have to make sure that the 'Leave image at the original location' box is checked. By clicking on the OK button you will now place the image into the left-hand cell.

Once the image has been inserted you will notice that the text in the right-hand cell has become vertically aligned in the middle of the cell (i.e. to the centre of the height of the image). This is

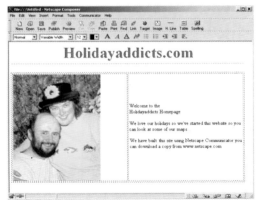

Fig. 15

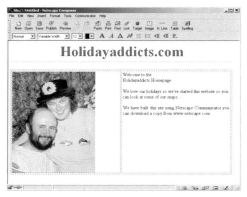

Fig. 16

because the default alignment of the cell is set to horizontally align the text to the left and vertically align it in the middle of the cell (fig. 15).

You can change the way the text is aligned in the cell by moving the cursor into the right-hand cell and bringing up the Cell Properties (Table info for Macs), as you did when you set the cell's width. When the box appears you can specify how both the Horizontal and Vertical Alignment are set. Click within the Vertical Alignment option on the Top button and click OK. This will then align the text at the top of the cell, and make it look more appealing for the user browsing the page (fig. 16, page 83). You can style the text within the right-hand cell. Using the same methods that we used to style the title text, you can apply any styles that you wish. For our page we have highlighted the first line within the table, increased its font size to 18 and made the text bold. We have then selected the remaining text and made its font size 14. Follow the same procedure and your table should then look like fig. 17.

Fig. 17

Fig. 18

6. You can now start adding links to the page. The first link you are going to create is a link to another website. You will notice in our text that we mention another site, **www.netscape.com**. The next task is to create a link so that if anyone clicks on this text, the browser locates this page on the Internet and opens it in its window.

First, highlight **www.netscape.com** (as this is the text we want to link). Once the text is highlighted, click on the Link icon in the toolbar. This will then bring up a Character Properties box, which you can use to specify where this text links to (fig. 18, page 85).

You will see that Netscape Composer puts the highlighted text in the top box under the heading Linked Text (indicating that this is the text to be used); you will then see an empty space, under 'Link to a page location or local file'. This is where

Naming your home page

Your home page must usually be named either **home.htm, home.html, index.htm** or **index.html**. This is because these names are ones that an Internet server recognizes, as default, as those for the home page of a website. Unless someone has a dedicated web address to visit (e.g. **www.holidayaddicts.com/venice.htm**) they will generally type the domain (e.g. **www.holidayaddicts.com**) into the browser. The browser then questions the Internet server for one of the four file names listed above to be you can input the full Internet address of the page that you want to link to. In this space, type in the full web address of the page. In this case, we've linked to **http://www.netscape.com**.

This will create a 'hyperlink' from the highlighted text. When you have done this, click OK and the changes will be made in your page.

displayed as the home page, thereby ensuring that anyone typing the address will be given the home page, unless they type in a particular page address. If this wasn't so, people would have to give out longer addresses, such as **www.holidayaddicts.com/myhomepage.htm** for people to reach the home page and there would be no consistency between sites for visitors to find the home page. Even worse, there would be no way of even finding a website without knowing the exact name of one of the pages. Always check with your webspace provider what it should be before constructing your website!

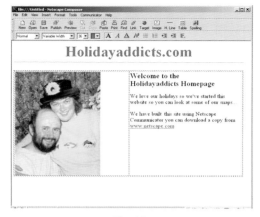

Fig. 19

You will notice that the text that you highlighted has changed colour and is now underlined (fig. 19). This is to indicate that this is a hyperlink. Well done, you have just created your first link!

7. The last thing to do before saving your page is to enter some details about the page. These details can include title, author, and description of the page and keywords associated with it. You can enter this information in a quick and easy-to-use window, rather then working out the HTML code and where it should be placed.

Find the Format menu and select the option Page Colors and Properties (PC) or Page Properties (Macintosh). A window will open to allow you to input the required information (fig. 20).

We will now enter general information

Fig. 20

regarding the page. This information creates the META Tags that are hidden away in the Head (top) of the page. If you want people using search engines to find your page, this is the place to put your keywords, which will be referenced by the search engines. For our sample holiday website, it's a good idea to put relevant words such as 'holiday', 'vacation', 'Egypt' and 'Venice' under the heading Keywords, but 'addicts' would not be such a good idea, as it may bring up your page in listings that aren't appropriate. You can always add other words you think are relevant, such as 'sun' and 'fun'.

8. You can now save the web page into the folder that you have created. Under the File menu you will see the option Save. When you are greeted with the Save dialog box, you can now name your page. As you have just created your home page, call it **home.htm** or whatever your host requires. It is recommended that for a file name you use something that represents its contents, so that it is easy for you to tell what the file contains when you come back to it later. However, the naming of your home page is crucial (see panel 'Naming your home page' on pages 86–87). When you have entered the filename, find the folder **webpages** that you created earlier and save your document there. As mentioned previously, different hosts may require a particular name for your home page.

Well done! You have successfully created your first web page!

9. The next step is to create a dedicated page about a vacation in Venice. To do this you will use most of the skills you used when you created the home page. The page that you are going to create will eventually look like fig. 21 (page 92).

This page contains text, images, horizontal lines and buttons, all of which were created in the home page. We will start our second page in the same way that we created our first page, by creating a blank page in Composer. This is achieved by going to the Communicator menu and selecting Composer, or by going to the File menu and choosing New, then

Fig. 21

Blank Page from the sub-menu.

A blank web page will appear and you can start typing in the information you require on the page. For the purposes of this tutorial, type 'Venice'. Next, you are going to make the title bigger in size and colour the text in red as you did on the home page.

To do this, highlight the word Venice and use the Text Size box. With the text highlighted, click on the size and select 36. This will then change the size of the type. With the text still highlighted, click on the Text Colour icon and select a new colour for your text (as shown in figs 7, 8 and 9). (For consistency, we have chosen the colour red again for our sample page.)

10. After styling the title text, add a horizontal line underneath it. To do this, place your cursor after the text and press Return once to create a new line. Once the cursor is on the new line, click on the Horizontal Line icon in the toolbar. This will insert the horizontal line under the title. You can then

apply style to this line in the same way that you did for your first page, as shown in fig. 10 (page 75).

Once the horizontal line is added the page will look like fig. 22.

11. The next stage is to add more detail about the Venice vacation, by adding pictures and text to the page.

After your horizontal line, press Return a couple of times to move your cursor to a new line. Once it is on the new line, you can type in your introductory text. After you have entered

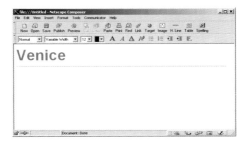

Fig. 22

the text you may style it by changing features such as the font, the size or the colour. Again, to do this, first highlight the text you want to change. With the text highlighted you can use the toolbar to change the attributes, just as you did for the title. (We have chosen to set the body copy on the vacation pages in the typeface Arial at size 12.)

Once you are happy with the look of the text you have just typed and styled, you can insert the first picture. Place your cursor at the end of your text and press Return a couple of times to move it to a new line. Once it is on the new line, you can place the image on to the page by clicking on the Image icon in the toolbar. Once you have clicked on the button, the Image Properties box appears for you to choose which picture you would like to insert (fig. 14, page 80). Follow the same principle as you did for inserting the image on the home page. By using the Choose File button in the window, you can find the image that you wish to use – in this case it's a photo of the Rialto Bridge taken from a vaporetto, named **bridge.jpg**. Once you have found the image, click OK in the first window. Once again, if you haven't changed the default preferences and want to retain your organized folder hierarchy, don't forget to check 'Leave image at the original location' before

Fig. 23

clicking on the OK button in the next window.

By clicking OK in the Image Properties window, the picture will then be inserted on the page where your cursor was placed. To finish this mini-section off, add a caption for the picture and then place another horizontal line across the page to section it off. Press Return to get the cursor under the picture, type in the caption and format the text as before. Then, place your cursor on a new line (by pressing Return). Once on the new line, click the Horizontal Line button in the toolbar and insert your line. After you have inserted and styled the line, your page should now resemble fig. 23.

12. The principles are the same as for the first page, but instead of putting the image and text inside a table we are placing the items directly on to the page. You can continue to add more text and pictures continuing down the page, repeating the same procedures. The remaining three pictures we have placed are, in order, **main_canal.jpg**, **side_canal.jpg** and **main_square.jpg**.

13. We should now save our Venice page. Under the File menu you will see the option Save. Move your cursor down the menu and select this option. You will then be given a Save dialog box. From here find the **webpages** folder that you originally created. Once you have located this folder, save your completed page as **venice.htm**.

On a PC

If you have not specified the Page Title in the Page Properties, you will be greeted with the Page Title window (fig. 24). Communicator will want you to title your page before saving. Once you have entered a title for your web page, click on OK to confirm.

Fig. 24

On a Mac

The title you give the file is automatically entered into Page Title if you have not already titled it. If you want to change the Page Title, you do this by going to the Format menu and choosing Page Title or Page Properties, then General.

14. The next stage in this tutorial is to complete a page to display information about a Nile cruise vacation in Egypt. This page will be very similar to the page of the Venice trip. It will use the same layout and format; the only difference will be the text and images you are going to use. The page is created in exactly the same way as the Venice page, using the pictures **ms_tut.jpg**, **kom_ombo_pillars.jpg**, **tomb_ceiling.jpg** and **karnak_statues.jpg**, in that order. When you have added all the information you should have a page that looks like fig. 25 (page 100). As before, now save your page in the **webpages** folder, under the title **egypt.htm**.

Fig. 25

15. The next stage is to create navigation bars on the pages, so that visitors can find their way around the website. To do this, we are going to use graphic buttons that we have already created for our navigation bar. (Alternatively, you could use text links. These would be based around the process detailed at stage 6 for creating the previous link.) If you didn't keep the home page open, you will need to load it into Composer.

On a PC

Go to the File menu and choose the option Open – Page. You will then be given an Open Page window (see fig. 26, page 102), which you can use to find the file that you created. Locate the file home.htm by clicking on Choose File and click OK. This will return you back to the Open Page window. Before opening the file, ensure that the button next to the Composer option is selected, otherwise your page will open into the browser and not into Composer! Clicking on Open opens the file so that you can work on it.

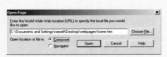

Fig. 26

On a Mac

A sub-menu from Open in the File menu offers you the choice to open either a Location or a Page in either Navigator or Communicator. Choose Page in Composer and then find the file home.htm, which you saved earlier.

Now you are going to place a graphic for a navigation button directly on to the page. Position your cursor after the table you created earlier and press Return. This should take you down to the next line. Now click on the Image icon in the toolbar, and select the graphic you wish to use as the first button. In our case this will be the home page button, named **home_button.gif**. Although this page actually is the home page, and so doesn't really need a navigation button to get to it, it's common practice for a navigation bar to be the same on every page throughout a website, for consistency. So, on any particular page, there may be a redundant button. Some sites will make this button look different, perhaps in a different colour, to indicate to the visitor that this is the page they are currently viewing.

After you have chosen the image file, and checked the 'Leave image at the original location' box (if required), click on the OK button. This will then insert the button on to the page (fig. 27, page 104). You can choose the position of the button to be on the left, centre or right of the page, by selecting the Paragraph option and choosing the desired alignment option.

You can now create the link for this button. Double-clicking on the button will bring up the Image Properties box (Format on a Mac). From here you will see a Link tab at the top of the

Fig. 27

window. Clicking on this will bring up the Link settings (fig. 28, page 105). You will notice that Netscape has listed the image that you had inserted as the Link source (Linked Text, on Macs even when it's a graphic). You are now going to instruct Composer to configure the link so that if

Fig. 28

anyone clicks on that image your home page will be loaded into their browser.

If you click on the Choose File button it will bring up the Open dialog window and you can now locate the page we created. Find your **webpages** folder, and select the file **home.htm**. You now return back to the Link property box, where you will notice Composer has added **home.htm** into the box. We could have typed this link in manually, but that might have resulted in mis-spellings. It is more reliable to click and find the file, as Composer will insert the correct name. As your experience and confidence grows, you may prefer to type the link straight in. To do this, simply click the cursor into the field and type **home.htm**.

Finally, when you click the OK button, Composer will attach the correct code to the button to link it to the chosen file. Now you need to repeat the same process for the buttons to link to the Venice and Egypt pages, selecting the relevant files saved earlier.

16. For the last button, you are going to create an e-mail link for the page, so that when a user clicks on this button, the Internet browser will automatically open the user's default e-mail software and create a new e-mail message addressed to the person specified on the button.

You will create the link in the same way that you created the links for the other buttons, but instead of finding a file to link to (or typing in the file's name) you are going to put the following into the link box:

Please note

On a Macintosh it is important that you create the buttons followed by their respective links as described. Because of a bug in the software, if you create a row of buttons first, then try to link them, you will have problems – Composer will not see the graphics as individual items and a link you make to one of the buttons will be attached to all the others on that line! You will only be able to target the same file from all the different buttons, unless you want to go into the raw HTML and edit it! (As an alternative work-around, you can place the buttons, each on a different line, make the links, then remove the Returns to place them on the same line.)

Another problem on a Mac is that you must place the image, OK it and then go back into the Image Format to make the link. If you try to make the link at the same time as placing the image, Composer will give you the file path as linked text followed by an unlinked image, duh! PC users do not have these problems...

mailto:info@holidayaddicts.com

The 'mailto:' section tells the browser to launch the user's e-mail software and create a blank e-mail. The information that follows it is the e-mail address where the e-mail will be sent. You can put any e-mail address in here, providing it's a valid e-mail address. Your Properties box should look something like fig. 29.

You have now successfully finished creating the navigation buttons and the links for them on the

Fig. 29

home page. Your page should now look like fig. 30 (page 110). You can preview your page in Netscape to see what the finished page looks like. To do this, click on the Preview icon (PC) ('View in Navigator' on a Mac) in the toolbar. Netscape will automatically load the page for you to see. You can perform this preview at any stage of the page design.

When you have finished any adjustments to your page, you can close the document window if you wish, although Composer will let you have several open at the same time, which may help if you are working on several interlinked pages at once. To see what the page looks like in HTML code, select Page Source from the View menu. This will then display the raw HTML code (including all the Tags) in a separate window (fig. 31). You won't see all the HTML code in this window, as some lines are too long for the window, but you can scroll along to see them on the screen.

17. The next task is to insert the navigation bar at the

Fig. 30

bottom of the Venice vacation page, and follow the same layout created for the home page by inserting the four graphical buttons with their links one after the other, exactly as you did on the home page (fig. 27, page 104, and fig. 30).

Once you have finished the navigation bar, the complete page will look like fig. 21 (page 92). You wouldn't see the page like this within the browser, as you would have to scroll down the page to see it all. We have pieced it together to give you an idea of what the whole finished page looks like. Now that the page has been created, you will need to save it, using the same process you followed when you saved the home page.

Follow the same procedure to place and enable the navigation bar buttons on the Egypt page. You can test the links by previewing your pages within

Fig. 31

the browser. You can then click on the buttons and they will open the page that you have linked them to.

Adding a download page

1. We have added the source files to the Holidayaddicts.com website for you to download. You may also wish to add files to your website for visitors to download.

   If you add a link to a file type that an Internet browser recognizes (e.g. a GIF or JPG picture file, or text file), it will open the linked file in the browser window and display its contents. Therefore, in order for files to be downloadable, they need to be of a type that cannot be opened by a browser. It is best to archive (or compress) them. This serves two purposes. Firstly, it ensures that the file is as small as possible, which means that it will download fairly quickly. Secondly, the browser isn't able to open compressed files, so instead of opening the file into a window, it gives the user the option to save the file to their hard drive – thus creating a download link.

To create a download page you will follow the same principles that have been covered so far in the tutorial – creating a page, adding some text and creating links. The only additional part is to create the archived (compressed) file.

2. Start the download page in the same way that you created the other pages, by creating a blank page in Composer. To do this, go to the Communicator menu and select Composer or go to the File menu and choose New, then Blank Page from the sub-menu. A blank web page will then appear and you can start typing in the information you require on the page.

In our example, we have once again typed **Holidayaddicts.com**. We have also opted to make the title bigger in size and colour the text in red and centre it, as we did on the home page. After styling the title text, we have added a horizontal line underneath the text.

Fig. 32

Once we added the horizontal line we typed in the text for the body of the download page. We have styled the body text in the same way as we did for the Venice and Egypt pages, but this time we've left it in the default variable-width font with the sub-heading 'Download Source Files' at size 18 and the remainder of the text at size 14. We have also centred all the text on the page. We have then created a navigation bar at the bottom of the page so that users can navigate from this page to the rest of the site if they wish. This was created in exactly the same way as the previous pages but, because it follows the centred text on the page, it is also centred by default (see fig. 32).

The next stage is to create the link so that the file can be downloaded. This link is created in the same way as those to pages and for the e-mail address, but instead of pointing the link to an HTML file it will be pointed to the archive file.

3. Before creating the link, make sure that you have created an archive file that contains the file (or files) that you want the visitor to download. This

Fig. 33

can be done with WinZip on a PC (available at **www.winzip.com**) or ZipIt on a Macintosh (available from **www.shareware.com**). Although Macintosh users are more familiar with Stuffit SIT files, PC users use ZIP files and these can also be decoded by Stuffit and Stuffit Expander, so if you save your file as a ZIP file it will be able to be decoded by users of both platforms. Within the **webpages** folder, create another folder (we've called it **source**) and save the archived file into this folder. (For this tutorial, we have chosen the name **archive.zip** for the file.)

Fig. 34

4. To create the link, highlight the words 'click here' on the page (see fig. 33, page 115) and click on the Link icon in the toolbar. This brings up the Properties box so you can select which file you want to link to when a user clicks on it (see fig. 34).

When the Properties box appears you will notice that the words 'click here' appear in the box that is marked Linked Text. This confirms that the text you have highlighted will become the link. The next step is to select the file that the link will go to. To do this, click on the button Choose File. This will then open a dialog box that you can use to locate the archived file.

Attention PC users

Because Composer assumes that you want to link an
HTM (or HTML) file, it automatically sets the file type
it looks for to HTML Files. You need to change this to
look for All Files (*.*), so that you will be able to pick
up the archive file that you created (see fig. 35). Once
you have set the file type, you can double-click on the
source folder and then double-click on the file called
archive.zip. This will then return you to the Link
Properties window. Click on OK to create the link.

Fig. 35

Attention Mac users

In the same way that the PC assumes you are linking HTM files, the Macintosh will only let you see web-related documents (HTM, HTML, GIF, JPG etc.). But unlike with a PC, which you can fool into looking for different files, there is no way of doing this on a Macintosh. Instead, you will have to type the file path into the 'Link To' box. (Netscape would automatically place the file path there if you selected the file through the 'Choose file' button.)

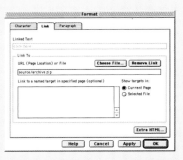

Fig. 36

The file path used should be from where the HTM file is saved, not the path to where it is on your entire hard drive! In other words, you would only need to type in **source/archive.zip** to link to the file that you saved in **source** folder earlier, not, for instance, **Macintosh HD/webpages/source/ archive.zip**. Once you have typed in the path, the Format window should look like fig. 36 (page 119). Clicking OK returns you to your page.

After you have returned to your page, the text 'click here' should now have changed to become blue in colour and underlined, indicating that this is a hyperlink (fig. 37).

Now that the link has been created, you can save the file in the same way as you did for the previous pages, but this time call the file **download.htm**.

Fig. 37

5. Having created and saved the download page, you now need to create a link to it from the home page, which you can do by adding another button to the navigation bar at the foot of the page.

First you will need to create the graphic, which you can then save into the **images** folder within your **webpages** folder. We have saved ours as **download_button.gif**. Now, if it's not still loaded into Composer, you need to open the home page as previously described. All you need to do is place the button in the navigation bar (on the same line as the other navigation buttons), then create the link.

As before, place the cursor after the last button, on the same line, and click on the Image icon in the toolbar. This brings up the Image Properties box (fig. 14, page 80). You can then click on Choose File to locate the image you wish to place. Find **download_button.gif** in the **images** folder and select it. Clicking OK returns you to the Image Properties box.

Before clicking OK, here's that warning again:

if you haven't changed the default preferences (and by now you'll wish you had!) and want to retain your organized folder hierarchy, don't forget to check 'Leave image at the original location' before clicking on OK. This will return you to the updated home page, which should look like fig. 5 on page 66.

Now you need to create the link. Either click on the button to highlight it, then click on the Link icon in the toolbar, which will take you directly to the Link settings; or double-click the button, which will take you to the Image Properties, where you will need to click on the Link tab. Once you have brought up the Link settings, click on Choose File, go to the **webpages** folder and select **download.htm,** the file you have just saved. Clicking OK returns you to the Link settings and you can now click OK and then save the file.

In the same way, you can add a button linking to the download page on to a navigation bar on any other page if desired.

Adding a background image/pattern

A background image or pattern is a commonly used feature on web pages, especially on non-commercial sites. This gives you the ability to add any image (GIF or JPEG) to replace the standard white background that is used on the page that we have created. The next stage, therefore, will be to add a background image to the download page.

The web page will take the image and tile it across the page, both vertically and horizontally, to fill the entire page. You have to be careful with the image you use, because it could mask out text that you have placed on the page. You also have to be careful that the image will tile properly. The right-hand edge of the image should fit with the left-hand edge, and the top should fit with the bottom. This is made easy if the edges of your image are all one single colour. Each page is treated independently and you can have a different background image on each page of your website.

For our sample page, we have created an image that resembles a watermark, using pale colours (fig. 38). This will ensure that it does not conflict with any text we have placed on our download page .

With the download page loaded into Composer, find the Format menu and select the option Page

Fig. 38

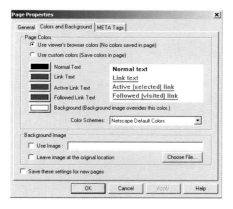

Fig. 39

Colours and Properties (PC) or Page Properties (Mac). When the Page Properties window appears, click on the Colours and Background tab at the top of the window that has just appeared (see fig. 39).

You will notice towards the bottom of the window the option of Background Image. By clicking on the Choose File button you will be

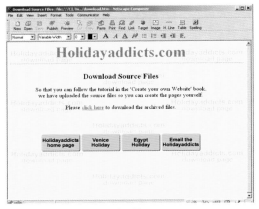

Fig. 40

greeted with the Open File window (the same window, which works by the same principle of inserting images, that you have encountered on previous pages). Find the file that you wish to use as your background. For our sample page, we have already saved a file called **back_ground.gif** in our **images** folder, located in the **webpages** folder.

Once you have located the file, click Open to return to the Page Properties window. You will notice that Netscape has entered the path of the file into the box for you. The last thing to do is to check the 'Leave image at the original location' checkbox if you haven't changed the default preferences and want to retain your organized folder hierarchy.

When you have done this, you can click on the OK button at the bottom of the window. This will then insert the chosen graphic file as the background to your page (see fig. 40, page 127).

You have now created your website, incorporating styled text, a table to facilitate layout, photographs, graphic buttons, links from text and graphics to other pages both within and beyond your own site, a background image and a download page. Your website is now complete . . . and ready for uploading to your Internet Service Provider's server!

UPLOADING
YOUR SITE

Uploading your site

Now that your site is complete and you have tested that all the images and buttons are correct and working, you will have to upload your finished pages and support files to your Internet Service Provider's (ISP) web server. This will enable people all over the world to view your new creation! First you will have to ensure that you have access to some web space (see 'Where can I find some web space?' on page 160). If you have already got your space, then you will need the details that should have been given to you by your 'host'. You should have a username and a password and have been told where to put the files. If you do not have these details, you will need to contact your host.

So far you have created all of your web pages and graphics within one folder stored on your computer, called **webpages.** You will need to transfer these to the web server using a process called FTP. FTP stands for 'File Transfer Protocol'. This is the Internet standard for transferring files from one computer to another. It also gives you the facility to manage the files once you have uploaded them to the web server, by allowing you to delete and rename files that have already been uploaded.

Most files are too large to be sent complete from one location to another; FTP breaks the file down into small, manageable pieces, then transfers them and reassembles the pieces at the other end into one complete file. The files can be text files, web pages or images. There are no restrictions on the type of file that can be transferred by FTP; it simply moves the information from one location to another.

Probably the most attractive feature of FTP is that it can be used through a graphical-based interface, allowing you to drag and drop the relevant file to the web server. Otherwise you would have to type in very long file path names and destinations to get your information to where it's required (e.g. **copy c:\mycomputer\myfiles\webpages\home.html**).

There are a number of FTP software packages available for both PCs and Macs and you may prefer to use a particular one, such as Cute FTP on the PC or Transmit on the Mac. Setting up the software you choose will depend on the way it is configured, so you will need to consult the documentation relevant to the package you choose. Many hosts have their own help files explaining how to upload to their servers using different popular packages.

As you can use Netscape to FTP the files to the server, we'll show you how to do it with Netscape. Please remember that from version 6 of Netscape Navigator onwards the upload facility is no longer enabled, and you will need to use either Communicator or an earlier version of Navigator.

Launch Netscape and instead of typing an Internet address, type in your personal information based upon the following criteria:

ftp://username:password@yourdomain

If you don't have your own domain, you will need to input the domain details required by your host.

Fig. 41

Netscape will then connect you to the FTP area, where you can start to upload the files that you have just created. Netscape will handle all of the communication and sending of passwords. You will be greeted with a screen similar to fig. 41.

Fig. 42

Uploading your site

Please note: Before uploading, check which folder (if any) your files have to be uploaded into. Your ISP may require them to be installed into a certain folder! If this is the case, simply click on the folder's name (within the Netscape window) to enter it.

There are now two ways of uploading your files to your FTP area:

1. You can simply drag your files and folders from within your **webpages** folder and drop them on to the open window. Netscape will then transfer all of the files selected up to your web space.

2. From the File menu you can choose the option Upload File. You can then select your files.

A message will then appear asking you to confirm that you want to upload the selected files (fig. 42). When you click on OK, Netscape will upload your files. A window will then appear detailing the progress of the files being copied.

When complete, your window should look like fig. 43.

Fig. 43

Your site is now uploaded and ready for the world to see! You can check that your site is working correctly by entering its web address in your browser window, as you would to visit any other site on the Internet.

Publish Icon

Although you can publish (upload) your page or
site through the Publish icon in the Composer
toolbar or via File menu, Publish, we would advise
you to use the FTP method described. The main
reason for this is that the FTP route allows you to
replace a single file that has changed or to create
additional folders within your web space. You
may, however, use Publish if you prefer.

ADVANCED **S**TUFF

Tables

You are limited to the layout tools available with HTML editing, in a way that you are not with desktop-publishing software. You can justify text left, right and centre, but if you want to start putting text into columns and structuring your page you will have to use tables. A table is basically a grid into which you can add rows, columns and cells. Rows go across a table, columns go up and down it and cells occur at the intersection of a row and a column. (See diagram.) If you've used spreadsheet software (e.g. Microsoft Excel), you'll understand the concept.

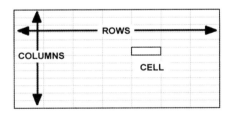

You can specify a table border. This places a line around the edge of each row and column, giving each cell an outline. You can also specify border colours and widths. As you can with text, you can specify a cell's horizontal and vertical alignment, thus controlling its contents. If you are preparing a table of figures, you could specify that the text titles are left aligned and the figures are right aligned, as in the example below.

Northern Sales	160,000
Eastern Sales	50,000
Southern Sales	275,000
Western Sales	15,000
Total Sales	**500,000**

You can also specify how a table is sized. There are two ways to do this. Firstly, you can set the width of the table to a specified percentage of the browser window. This can be useful, as you can't know the resolution (width) of the user's computer screen (in pixels). The second method of sizing a table involves using pixels. You can fix the width of the table to a certain size; then no matter what the user resizes their window to, the table width will not change. Another useful table feature is the ability to colour the background of each cell or to display an image as the background.

There is nothing to stop you 'nesting' one table inside another. There is no limit on how many tables you can 'nest' within other tables. This method gives you even more control over structuring your page. Tables are an extremely powerful tool in developing your web pages. To master tables will involve facing a challenging learning curve, but if you want to produce a sharp-looking website, then you will have to navigate it. WYSIWYG editors make table-editing a lot easier than trying to build them in raw HTML Tag form. Just remember to plan your table by making a sketch on paper, play around with ideas and take your time. If it doesn't work, then you can always delete your table and start again!

Hit counters

A hit counter tracks (or counts) the number of people who visit your web page. This allows you to gauge how many people visit your site each day, week or year.

Hit counters are generally based around a CGI Script (see later for further information on this) and are based on an Internet web server. The script simply takes the existing number of visits your website has already had and then increases it by one each time your home page is requested by a user to be viewed in their Internet browser. Depending on what or whose counter you use, the results can be presented in plain text or as graphical information, showing numbers, dates and times of when your website was 'hit' (accessed by a visitor).

Advanced stuff

Your ISP may already have the CGI Script available for you to use. Alternatively, you can get third parties to provide you with the service. Hit counter information can be found at:

> www.bravenet.com
> www.easycounter.com
> www.beseen.com

With any of the above services you can select the type of counter you would like (graphic- or text-based) and the style in which you would like it to be displayed (e.g. the colours you would like, or the styles of typeface). You may even choose to keep your counter invisible – that way you can track how many people are looking at your site but other people will remain unaware of the number. This can be handy if the number is embarrassingly low! After you have decided on the format that you would like your counter to take, your hit-counter provider will then supply you with the appropriate HTML code to include within your web page. No programming or server-side configuration is required; you simply copy and paste the code into your document.

You might want to have different counters on different pages within your site. In the case of Holidayaddicts.com, we might want to insert a hit counter on our home page so that we can see how many people have discovered our site, but at the same time we could place separate hit counters on both our Venice and Egypt pages. This would then give us a breakdown of which pages the users viewed once they were on our site.

Frames

HTML enables you to use a technology called 'frames', which allows you to divide your page into multiple scrollable areas. This will enable a visitor to your site to open more than one web page in a single window. With a frameset, you build a structure for how the page will look and tell the browser which pages to open in a particular area. The most commonly used framesets are those of a navigation area and a content area for a page. Using framesets allows you to keep your navigation buttons to one side of the window, whilst only opening the relevant information page on the other side. You can also define a frameset so that the navigation section cannot be resized or moved. This can allow you to position the navigation bar alongside your document, so that the navigation buttons remain static while the page can be scrolled up and down.

You have to name each section, which means naming each frame. So, when a user opens a link from a framed page, the link tells the browser to open the required page into the named frame.

However, this functionality comes at a price. Frames can cause a number of problems, such as not displaying the correct page in the frame required. Moreover, many browsers do not offer the ability to print the frames as displayed. Furthermore, because you have to have a web page for the contents of a frame, a web-based search engine may just pick up the page but not the complete page holding the frame. If a visitor then searches for something on your site, and clicks through on the page found, it may not be displayed as you intend, i.e. the page that would have been framed is displayed, but no frames are displayed and there will be no navigation frame. This can also happen if a visitor goes back to a page via a browser's history or if they have 'bookmarked' it. There is no limit to the number of frames you can include on a page, but it can soon get confusing for the user if you have too many.

We would recommend that any newcomers to Internet design do not use frames, as it requires a lot of thought and experience to ensure that links and naming are correct. Even experienced web designers are advised to use frames as sparingly as possible!

Forms

Forms allow you to collect information from the visitor viewing your website. Common uses for forms include order forms, surveys, information requests, catalogue requests and search interfaces.

Forms consist of two components. The first is the HTML code, or the page into which the user enters all the information. The second is either an application that sits on your web server or a script that is built into the page. This allows the processing of the information that the user inputs into your form. Mostly, the information is e-mailed directly to the owner of the website, but you can store and record the information from a form into a database.

Forms can include elements such as text fields, buttons, checkboxes, radio buttons, lists and menus, to name but a few.

Hidden elements

Hidden elements are invisible items that are included within your web page for functionality but are not seen by the user browsing the page. The user can choose to see the elements, however, by going to Page Source, which displays the raw HTML code.

Examples of some common hidden elements are listed below.

Meta Tags

Meta Tags allow information about the content of your page to control your listing in some search engines. They provide an easy way for search engines to catalogue your page through keywords and descriptions. Meta Tags do not guarantee to boost your page's rating within a search engine listing, but they can help.

Meta Tags are placed in the head of the page. Some web-creation software allows you to add Meta Tags through a menu option. The software lets you type your information in and automatically creates the Tags. The two main uses for Meta Tags are:

Keywords

This allows you to insert common words that a user might use when searching for information. Please remember that you are inserting these keywords to make up for the lack of text on your pages. It is impossible to think of every variation that a user may input to search for your page. Keep your keywords precise and relevant to your page. The more specialist the keywords are, the better chance there is that they will find you. For example, if you can't register your company name or your own name as a top-level domain, you can at least put it in the keywords! You might also want to include common misspellings of any easily misspelt words.

Description

This allows you to insert a description that the search engine page will use when displaying your web page as one of its results. Again, be precise about what your page contains, as it's probably the first time a user will have come across your site. Keep the description short as well – users will soon pass over your site if the description is long-winded.

Named anchors or targets

Named anchors (or targets) allow you to set positional place markers in a web page. If you were creating a large web page that would normally fill up three or four pages, you could insert anchors throughout the page to make the navigation easier for the user. For example, if you were creating a products page to hold twenty products (with a picture, title and description for each item), you may have a small menu at the top of your page listing the different products available (such as an index). You could then insert an anchor (or target) at the start of each product going down the page (each anchor must have its own individual name). You would then create a link from the menu listing at the top of the page to the appropriate anchor. This would enable the user to click on the item of interest, whereupon the browser would automatically jump to the correct product, rather than the user having to scroll through pages of information to find it.

Scripts

These are normally JavaScripts (see later for further information), inserted into the web page for functionality at the user's end. Scripts might be used to show the current date and time or to add up numbers in a table column. If you are designing a dynamically driven website, then you might use VB (Visual Basic) Script rather than JavaScript. The primary difference between JavaScript and VB Script is that JavaScripts are set to run tasks or procedures at the client (user's) end, while VB Scripts generally run tasks or procedures at the Internet Service Provider's end.

JavaScript

JavaScript code can be added to your web page to create interactive documents. As a result, JavaScript is often used to create interactive Web-based forms. All modern browsers have JavaScript support built into them as standard. JavaScript is a relatively simple-to-comprehend, easy-to-use scripting language. Although you will need a small amount of experience to program JavaScript, many sites are available that offer pre-written scripts for you to copy and paste into your document. Examples of these can be found at **www.javascript.com** and **www.jsworld.com**.

JavaScript can be used in web pages to insert calculators for forms, to display the date and time on a web page and to supply the facility to verify information that a user enters into a form. For example, it may be used to check that the number entered as a credit card number is not just a random sequence of numbers!

Comments

Comments can be added so that you can set little reminders on the web page (e.g. you can place an HTML comment to indicate that the content begins from a set point). Comments add no functionality to the web page for the user.

Image maps

With an Image map you can specify which web page (or link) opens, depending on the area the user clicks on. For example, you might have a map of the world displayed on your web page and want a different web page to open if someone clicks on the United States of America from the one that would open if someone clicks on the United Kingdom. An image map would let you configure the world map so that a different page opens depending on the area that the user clicks on.

Other hidden elements can include line breaks, hidden form fields, form delimiters, Cold Fusion Tags

(CFM) and Advanced Server Tags (ASP).

Dynamic sites

Although you can build your pages in HTML, those pages remain static and the only way of updating them is for you to change the page yourself. This may be as simple as adding some new lines of text, but if you plan to put a catalogue of products on the Web this could be a very long-winded process.

The solution to this is to build a dynamic site! Firstly, you place all of your data in a database. Then, when a user requests the information from your website, the web page questions the database for the required information. The database returns this information to the web page, which displays to the user via the web browser. Using this method, additional information can be included on a website very quickly and easily, without the need to create or modify any pages.

There are many types of terminology associated

with dynamic sites – you might have seen some of them yourself while surfing the Net. Pages with web file names that end **.asp**, **.php**, **.cfm** or **.ibc** are all types of dynamically driven sites.

CGI Scripts

We have taken you through building your website in HTML. For basic usage of text and images this technology is fine, but if you want to add interactivity and extend your page then you will have to look at something like CGI. CGI stands for 'Common Gateway Interface' and allows data passed from the user's browser back to the web server to be processed by another program on the web server computer. The server can then pass the program's results back to the browser, having decided what information to display next.

CGI Scripts can be written in a number of different programming languages. Every CGI script must be customized to a certain extent in order to run on a particular server. There are two ways to develop

CGI Scripts. The first is to create your script from scratch; the second is to modify an existing script. The second is a much easier approach, as there is probably a script already available that someone has written which you can modify for your requirements.

CGI Scripts and resources can be found at the following sites:

www.cgiscriptcenter.com
www.cgi-resources.com
www.cgi-world.com
www.freecentre.net

You will need to ensure that the web server your site is hosted by is capable of running CGI Scripts. Normally scripts will be saved and stored within a folder called **cgi-bin**. Once you have written (or modified) the scripts, you will have to set the permissions on the file so that it can be read/written to and/or executed and by whom (further details on this will be available from your host). The final task is to call the CGI script from your web page.

The most common use of a CGI script is to e-mail back information that a user has entered into a form.

DHTML

Dynamic Hypertext Markup Language (DHTML) is the latest development in creating web pages. Whereas HTML is based around 'static' pages, DHTML allows you to make dynamic applications to elements on your web page. These features are generated from the browser rather than by any processing on the web server.

DHTML enables you to perform actions such as animating objects so that they can move around the page, and to use layers so that pictures can be placed in front of one another and make items change (e.g. changing the colour of text) when the user moves the mouse over them (an action known as a 'rollover').

This only scratches the surface of what DHTML can achieve. But it will only work with version 4 browsers upwards and there are still incompatibilities. One of the most commonly used features of DHTML is Cascading Style Sheets.

Cascading Style Sheets

CSS, or Cascading Style Sheets, give many advanced features to you while developing your web pages. They control a number of characteristics on the actual web page, such as alterations to existing HTML Tags or the creation of new Tags.

With CSS you can specify, for example, that a certain HTML Tag should be displayed in a Verdana typeface at 24 points and coloured red. Whenever you use that Tag on the page, the type will be in that style. CSS can be applied to an individual web page or to a whole site if required. This means that you can set up a corporate style for your site. For example, if you were building an online catalogue and wanted all of the products in your catalogue to be displayed in a certain way (e.g. the title of the product in Times, 14 point, bold and coloured green and the description of the product in Helvetica, 10 point, coloured black) you could create these characteristics as a new Tag and only specify that Tag when building catalogue pages.

There are many useful features about CSS, but they do have their drawbacks. Some browsers do not understand CSS and do not use them (even if you have specified that they are to be used), so caution should always be exercised. Further detailed information about CSS can be found at:

> www.mako4css.com/
> www.w3.org/Style/CSS/
> www.htmlhelp.com/reference/css/

Where can I find some web space?

You may have built your website, but you will need to upload it for the world to see. You may already have some free web space available from your Internet Service Provider. Many ISPs include this space as part of their package, along with e-mail and Internet accessibility. Apple Computer's **mac.com** even provides the facility for you to build a simple site online. Please check with your provider to see how much space you have (if any!).

If you plan on having a large, busy site, then most providers will want to charge you a business rate, possibly based on the amount of traffic your site will generate (another good reason why you should keep file sizes small!).

If your provider does not give you any space, then you can rely on third parties to host your site. Some providers charge for this. There are a number of free providers available, although most of them will put banner adverts on your page and some may place restrictions on what you can do.

Here are a few:

> www.geocities.com
> www.tripod.com
> www.directNIC.net
> www.mac.com
> www.theglobe.com

Creation software

Although we have built our pages with the Composer part of Netscape Communicator, there is a host of software packages with which you can build web pages. Some are commercially based packages, while others are shareware (software that you can try out before you buy). Pricing will vary according to what the packages offer.

In this section we have listed a few web page creation packages that are currently available. Most can be downloaded from the vendor's website for you to try, free, for a limited period. Trial versions are also often available on the free CDs that come with computer magazines.

WYSIWYG HTML editors

Macromedia Dreamweaver, Macintosh and PC,
www.macromedia.com

Adobe Golive, Macintosh and PC,
www.adobe.com

Netscape Communicator, Macintosh and PC,
www.netscape.com

HTML code editors

Allaire Homesite, PC only,
www.allaire.com

BB Edit, Macintosh only,
www.barebones.com

Graphics editors

Macromedia Fireworks, Macintosh and PC,
www.macromedia.com

Adobe PhotoShop, Macintosh and PC,
www.adobe.com

Adobe PhotoDeluxe, Macintosh and PC,
www.adobe.com

Corel Graphics Suite, Macintosh and PC,
www.corel.com

Multimedia editors

Macromedia Flash, Macintosh and PC,
www.macromedia.com

Adobe Live Motion, Macintosh and PC,
www.adobe.com

These software titles are just a few of the mainstream
applications available to help you design and create

your website. There are many freeware titles (software that you can download and use free of charge) and shareware titles available. Shareware and freeware can often be found on computer magazine CDs and you can search for them on a number of websites, including the following:

www.shareware.com

www.download.com

www.macshare.com

www.zdnet.com

Maintaining your site

So you have built your site, uploaded it and told the world that your site exists! What else is there left to do? The next task that faces you is to make sure that you update your site on a regular basis. If you are using your site to promote your business or products, it is important to keep it updated. There is nothing worse for a visitor than returning to a site after a couple of months and seeing no change to the information on it. You can make your changes offline, review them on your computer and then update the relevant pages.

WAP

WAP (Wireless Application Protocol) is a standard protocol that allows specially prepared Internet content to be accessed by mobile phones, personal organizers and pagers. Obviously, this has to be pretty much text-based and requires special versions of websites.

Most networks now offer their own portals (literally doorways through which the user can move on to something else) for WAP users and there are others available. You may now even be able to access your bank account from your WAP-enabled phone (depending on your bank).

To access the Internet via WAP you will need a

WAP phone, a connection to a digital network, a WAP service provider and a data-enabled SIM card. There are more and more handsets coming onto the market now that are WAP enabled and soon WAP may become a standard feature.

PDAs (Personal Digital Assistants) can also be used to access WAP services, using extra software and a mobile phone. The phone doesn't have to be WAP enabled, it must simply be able to link up to a PDA and to use the GSM data service – most mobile phones can do this.

While WAP can be pretty useful now – offering access to information whenever and wherever you are – the Mobile Internet is set to evolve in many ways over the next few years. The crucial factors affecting its growth will be the speed at which data can be transferred, screen quality, battery life and the development of applications.

The future

Now that the Internet as we know it has been swamped by surfers and commercial enterprises looking for any opportunity to make a profit from it, the educational and research establishments are looking for better alternatives. There are currently moves towards various kinds of 'super' Internet. In the USA, 180 universities, backed by the National Science Foundation and the US federal government, have put together Internet2, and have involved companies such as IBM and Cisco (who make most of the hardware that the Internet runs on). Internet2 is so fast and reliable that the telescopes on top of Mauna Kea in Hawaii connected to Internet2 can be controlled by astronomers from their computers back in their research labs.

Elsewhere, Geant, a super-fast network covering over 3,000 academic and research establishments in 32 countries, was launched on 1 December 2001 in Europe. Based around the UK, Germany, France and the Benelux countries, this system benefits from being developed more recently. It has a budget of 200 million euro over the next four years, of which 80 million euro comes from the European Commission. All these countries have their own national research networks, such as Janet (Joint Academic Network) in the UK. The speeds achievable on these networks – possibly up to 40 gigabits per second (a gigabit being 1 billion units of digital data) – make the existing Internet look like it's at a standstill by comparison. These super-fast networks use existing cabling, so perhaps eventually these facilities will become available to everybody.

And there is now also talk of VDSL (Very high bit-rate DSL), which, using standard copper telephone wires, is capable of transferring 14 megabits per second (a megabit being 1 million units of digital data), 28 times faster than ADSL. At the time of writing, users in the United States are only being offered 1 megabit per second on VDSL.

Ironically, although fibre-optic is supposedly the way to go, ADSL and VDSL will not run on fibre-optic cables. They are designed to get the best out of good old-fashioned copper telephone wires. Supposedly, there is a limit to the distance you can be from a telephone exchange if you are using Digital Subscriber Line technologies – 3.5 kilometres for ADSL (although RADSL can extend this to 5.5 kilometres) and about 800–900 metres for VDSL, but there is nothing to prevent telecom companies, if they have the will, from putting the VDSL boxes within the more localized boxes used for telephone distribution. Watch this space . . .

GLOSSARY

Glossary

@ – As used in an e-mail address, username@domain, e.g. joe@mydomain.

ADSL – Asymmetric Digital Subscriber Line. 'Asymmetric' because the upload speed is not as fast as the download speed, the theory being that most Internet users download a lot more than they upload, so the upload speed is compromised to give a greater download speed. Basic ADSL offers speeds up to 2,048 kilobits per second for downloads, as opposed to 256 kilobits per second upload. Some providers will offer download speeds up to 2 megabits per second, although the upload speed remains at 256 kilobits per second.

ASP – Active Server Pages. Web pages that are created dynamically by a web server containing HTML and scripting code. Under ASP, programs are run in a similar way to CGI Scripts. When the visitor to a site requests data from an Active Server Page, the server sends the HTML back to the browser.

bandwidth – The volume of data that can be sent through a connection, measured in bits per second. Often called the size of the 'pipe'.

bit – A single unit of digital data. 8 bits make up 1 byte.

bookmark – A web address stored by your web browser so you can return to it easily. Called a Favorite in Internet Explorer.

broadband – A high-speed Internet connection, such as ADSL, cable modem or leased lines, that can use more than one channel at a time to transfer data and hence transfer more data in a given period.

browser – The application software used to view web pages (e.g. Netscape or Internet Explorer).

byte – A computer 'word' made up of 8 bits.

cable modem – A modem that enables you to connect your computer to a cable TV line with a fast connection.

CGI – Common Gateway Interface. A protocol that enables a web server to run an application and to transfer the resulting information to your browser.

chatroom – A website where users 'chat' (by typing on a computer keyboard or using a microphone) with other people, usually with similar interests.

client – Another word for the computer or browser used by a website visitor.

CMYK – Cyan, Magenta, Yellow, blacK. The system of saving colour files for printing, as opposed to on a screen, on the Web. These are the colours used in full colour printing.

compression – The process of reducing the size of a file to save download time.

content – Information available on the Internet – what you see on web pages.

cookie – A small text file sent from a website to your hard disk containing information about your visit. It can be updated with each return visit. Cookies save information such as your login name, your password and which pages you accessed. Servers can only read their own cookies. You can turn cookies off in your browser, but some sites won't let you in if you do. Some sites use them to 'personalize' your 'experience' when you return.

CSS – Cascading Style Sheets. Part of DHTML, these make many advanced features available to you for the purpose of developing your web pages. They control a number of characteristics on the web page, and are useful when changing existing HTML Tags or creating new Tags.

database – A store of ordered data that can be retrieved as required. Most e-commerce and catalogue-type websites are driven from a database, as they are easier to update.

DHTML – Dynamic HTML. The name for an advanced version of Hypertext Markup Language (HTML) Tags and options, enabling you to create more animated web pages, which are more responsive to user interaction. Rollovers, CSS and layers are a few examples of DHTML. The main problem with DHTML is that it only works with version 4 browsers upwards (some features are still incompatible). As many users are still working with older browsers, two versions must be created of each website, serving the pages appropriate to each visitor's browser.

DNS – Domain Name Server. This translates domain names into IP addresses. Domain names are easier to remember, but the Internet runs on IP addresses (see later for a definition of these). Every time you use a domain name, therefore, a DNS must translate the name into the corresponding IP address. For example, the domain name **holidayaddicts.com** might translate to 66.79.10.214 as an IP address. If a DNS server can't translate a domain name, it passes the request on to another DNS server, and so on, until the correct IP address is found.

DSL – Digital Subscriber Line. The technology for bringing fast Internet connections to homes and small businesses over standard copper telephone lines. We now have ADSL, RADSL and VDSL.

e-commerce – Online business, usually the Internet equivalent of mail-order.

e-mail – Electronic mail.

form – An HTML element that sends data back to the server.

FTP – File Transfer Protocol. FTP is used to transfer files from one computer to another. You would use FTP to upload your web page from your computer at home to a web server so that visitors can look at it.

GIF – Graphics Interchange Format. Originally devised by CompuServe. A format used for compressed bitmap images. Generally considered best for graphic images, as opposed to photographic images. Essential for animations, or where transparency is required.

gigabit – A billion bits.

hit – Each time a visitor's browser requests a page element, it is recorded by the server as a 'hit'.

Hits are generated for each element of a requested page (including graphics, text, photographs and forms). If a page containing four graphics is viewed by a user, five hits will be recorded – one for the page itself and one for each graphic. Hits can be recorded by hit counters. These can be set to record just the number of visitors to a website rather than the number of elements downloaded.

home page – 1. The first or 'cover' page of a website. The home page often contains, or has links to, an index for the site. 2. The web page you see first each time you connect to the Web.

host – A computer connected to the Internet that acts as a server, allowing visitors to access files on it.

HTML – Hypertext Markup Language. A programming language that is used to make web pages. HTML facilitates links to other files or locations on the Internet.

HTTP – Hypertext Transfer Protocol. The protocol used between servers and browsers.

hyperlink – A graphic or text item on a website that, when clicked on, will take a user to a related, linked location. Text links usually will be shown underlined and often in a different colour (most often blue, usually turning purple after the link has been used once) from the rest of the text on the screen. A graphic link usually has a frame around it. The mouse pointer usually changes to a pointing hand when it is passed over a hyperlink.

hypertext – Text containing links which, when clicked on, take the visitor to a different place in the document or to another document.

Internet – Short for 'interconnected networks'. A global network connecting millions of computers. Over 100 countries are connected to the Internet. Also known as the Net.

intranet – A private network that may or may not be connected to the Internet, but that works in a similar way. Some companies set up servers on their own internal networks so employees have access to the company's private website.

IP – Internet Protocol. The protocol, or 'language', used for sending data around the Internet. The IP in TCP/IP.

IP address – Internet Protocol address. Every computer connected to the Internet has a unique IP address, which is a number in the format W.X.Y.Z, where W, X, Y and Z are numbers between 0 and 255 (inclusive). Generally, domain names are used instead of IP addresses and the domain name servers convert domain names into IP addresses.

IRC – Internet Relay Chat. A worldwide network of enthusiasts communicating with each other in real time. These chatrooms tend to be devoted to specialist interests.

ISDN – Integrated Services Digital Network. Now somewhat old technology, ISDN is a digital system that allows data transfer of 64Kbps per channel over a digital phone line. Channels can be paired, quadrupled and further grouped for higher speeds, but ISDN is archaic compared to ADSL or cable modems.

ISP – Internet Service Provider. A company providing access to the Internet, and to additional services on it.

JavaScript – A programming and scripting language. Used in website development to create interactive content on the Web.

JPEG – Joint Photographic Experts Group. A graphic image compression format. When you save a JPEG, you can choose the quality of the stored image. As the highest quality makes for the largest file, you generally have to strike a compromise between image quality and file size. Also referred to as a 'jpg'.

Kbps – Kilobits per second. A measure of how fast digital data can be sent down a phone line and therefore also a measure of your modem's speed. The fastest modems operate at 56Kbps, but most telephone lines can't support this and typical maximum modem speeds over ordinary telephone lines are 44–48Kbps.

kilobit – A thousand bits.

link – Short for 'hyperlink'.

Mbps – Megabits per second. See also Kbps.

megabit – A million bits.

modem – Short for modulator/demodulator. The device that converts digital data into analogue data, and vice versa, to send and receive it down a telephone line.

navigation bar – A graphic facility, often taking the form of a row of buttons or a panel, that enables the user to move conveniently from one page to another on a website. Also known as a Navbar.

newsgroup – A discussion group on Usenet devoted to exchanging information and ideas on a specific subject. At the moment there are tens of thousands of newsgroups. Not often much to do with news, they are ongoing discussion groups among Internet users who share a mutual interest.

operating system – The program in a computer that controls its basic functions. Windows (on a PC), Mac OS (on a Macintosh) and Linux, are all operating systems. Often referred to as OS.

page – Every website is a collection of pages, just as a magazine is a collection of pages joined together. Each web page is a document formatted in HTML that can contain text, images and other items.

PDA – Personal Digital Assistant. A palm-sized computer capable of connecting to the Internet; a step up from a personal organizer. Palm Computing leads the way, hotly pursued by Handspring and companies making Pocket PCs, such as Compaq. Apple's Newton was way before its time but, sadly, too large and not capable enough.

PDF – Portable Document Format. Devised by Adobe. A cross-platform format used mainly for previewing documents for print. Also a popular format for manuals and help files.

PDFs can be opened within a web browser, if you have the appropriate plug-in installed.

PHP – Pre-Hypertext Processor. A tool that lets you create dynamic web pages. PHP-enabled web pages are treated in the same way as normal HTML pages and can be created and edited in the same way.

platform – The operating system (Windows, Apple Mac, Unix) used by a computer.

plug-in – A small piece of software that adds functionality to a main software application.

portal – A gateway to other sites, or a general point of contact; a site that usually features lots of links, such as a home page for the provider, quite likely with a search engine as well. A good example of a portal is **www.netscape.com**.

RADSL – Rate-adaptive variation of Asymmetric Digital Subscriber Line. Also known as extended-reach ADSL, this works over distances up to 5.5km rather than the usual 3.5km restriction. In this variation, the upload speed is further compromised, down to as little as 64Kbps if necessary.

RGB – Red, Green, Blue. The colours that, when combined, produce full colour on a computer screen.

rollover – The effect in DHTML when moving the mouse over text or an object causes it to change.

search engine – A website that provides the facility for visitors to search for items in the content of other websites.

server – A computer providing services that clients on a network, such as the Internet, can access.

SIT – Stuffit compressed file (Macintosh format).

surfer – A visitor to a website, or an Internet user.

TCP/IP – Transmission Control Protocol/Internet Protocol. The standard way of moving data across the Net. TCP is the quality control system that checks the data transfer for errors, and ensures it arrives in the right order and is delivered to the right program. IP is the unique numerical address of each connected computer.

UNIX – A type of computer operating system, favoured by Internet servers and in academic institutions for its power, stability and flexibility.

URL – Universal – or Uniform – Resource Locator. The unique address of a site on the Internet. For example, **http://www.holidayaddicts.com** is the URL for the Holiday Addicts home page.

Usenet – A system of newsgroups that consists of thousands of conferences that people post messages to and which are updated around the world on a regular basis.

VDSL – Very high bit-rate Digital Subscriber Line. Speeds of up to 14 megabits per second.

WAP – Wireless Application Protocol. Protocol that enables mobile devices (mobile phones or PDAs) to connect to the Internet.

web browser – An application that enables the user to look at web pages and websites. Examples include Netscape, Internet Explorer and Opera.

Web Safe colours – A cross-platform colour palette of 216 colours. Normally the minimum colour palette that a computer uses is based around 256 colours, but different computer systems don't use the same 256 colours! The 216 that are 'Web Safe' are all used by the major operating systems, so all graphics created for the Web using the 216 can be displayed consistently between Windows, Macintosh and Unix platforms.

web server – A computer on the Internet that hosts web pages and makes them available for clients.

WWW – The World Wide Web. The WWW is what most people think of as the Internet, but in fact it is really only a part of it. Also known as W3 and the Web.

WYSIWYG – What You See Is What You Get (pronounced 'wizzywig'). Graphical design interface that does exactly what it says – lets you see exactly what you will get on screen.

Zip – To compress or archive files using WinZip, PKZIP, ZipIt, gzip, or another compatible archive program.

USEFUL SITES

Search engines

www.altavista.com

www.ask.co.uk

www.dogpile.com

www.excite.com

www.google.com

www.hotbot.com

www.lycos.com

www.yahoo.com

Shareware/Freeware

www.shareware.com

www.download.com

www.macshare.com

www.zdnet.com

Free web space

www.geocities.com

www.tripod.com

www.xoom.com

www.theglobe.com

www.directNIC.net

www.mac.com

Domain name registration

www.netnames.co.uk

www.interNIC.com

www.directNIC.net

Web graphics

www.clipart.com

www.freegraphics.com

www.arttoday.com

HTML/Website creation help

www.htmlgoodies.com

www.websitegoodies.com

www.websitegarage.com

curriculum.calstatela.edu/courses/builders/
lessons/less/lesintro/toolkit.html

www.hotwired.lycos.com/webmonkey

www.learnthat.com/courses/computer/
developer.shtml

www.webdesign.about.com/compute/webdesign

www.bfree.on.ca/HTML

Hit counters

www.bravenet.com

www.easycounter.com

www.beseen.com